Boundless

Boundless

Living life in overflow

Danielle Strickland
and
Stephen Court

MONARCH
BOOKS
Oxford, UK & Grand Rapids, Michigan, USA

Published by Monarch Books
an imprint of
Lion Hudson plc
Wilkinson House, Jordan Hill Road,
Oxford OX2 8DR, England
monarch@lionhudson.com
www.lionhudson.com/monarch

Published with The Salvation Army

ISBN 978 0 85721 451 5
e-ISBN 978 0 85721 452 2

First edition 2013

Acknowledgments
Scripture quotation marked Amplified Bible taken from the Amplified® Bible, Copyright
© 1954, 1958, 1962, 1965, 1987 by The Lockman Foundation. Used by permission.
Scripture quotations marked The Message taken from The Message. Copyright © by
Eugene H. Peterson 1993, 1994, 1995, 1996, 2000, 2001, 2002. Used by permission of
NavPress Publishing Group.
Scripture quotations marked New International Version taken from the Holy Bible,
New International Version Anglicised. Copyright © 1979, 1984, 2011 Biblica, formerly
International Bible Society. Used by permission of Hodder & Stoughton Ltd, an
Hachette UK company. All rights reserved. "NIV" is a registered trademark of Biblica.
UK trademark number 1448790.
Scripture quotations marked New Living Translation are taken from the Holy Bible,
New Living Translation, copyright © 1996, 2004, 2007 by Tyndale House Foundation.
Used by permission of Tyndale House Publishers, Inc., Carol Stream, Illinois 60188. All
rights reserved.
Scripture quotation marked New Life Version is taken from the New Life Version ©
Christian Literature International.
Scripture quotations marked God's Word Translation are taken from GOD'S WORD®,
© 1995 God's Word to the Nations. Used by permission of Baker Publishing Group.

A catalogue record for this book is available from the British Library

Printed and bound in the United States, March 2013, LH30

To Moses, Judah and Zion
You were born to change the world.
May you keep exploring the wonders
of the overflow in your lives.

Contents

Acknowledgments

William and Catherine Booth are incredible examples of living life in overflow – their boundless influence extends to both of us! We're grateful to The Salvation Army for its soul-saving mission, and to Tony Collins, Jenny Ward and the crew at Lion Hudson for making *Boundless* overflow.

1

A Tattoo, Salvation,
and a Song

*I*t took me about eight different tattoo parlours before I found the guy who would be willing to come with me to a large youth conference and give me a tattoo on stage. Actually, even him I had to coax to come. I was speaking, together with my husband, Stephen, to a crowd of teenagers about living life in a way we were meant to. On this day we were getting to covenant – this is living in promise, living with a purpose, living for something and someone larger than ourselves – and we were trying to communicate it to a generation that had been labelled selfish, fickle, and loose.

Tattoos can be a big deal. They are for ever. They are painful. They are obvious – and did I mention painful? So, in front of all these young people and many surprised older leaders I sat in the middle of the stage as my new tattooist friend started up his gun and began the work. My husband broke down the scriptural significance of living for something bigger than your own life, while I publicly endured the pain and embraced being marked for ever. The tattoo I chose was a song – it is the musical theme of this book, with words that a man named William Booth penned more than a century ago. It was about an idea that has completely changed the world. It wasn't Booth's idea – he just wrote about it and lived it out. It was God's idea – from the very beginning.

The world was meant to be good. Actually, when God created it He said it was beautiful (that's what "very good" means in Hebrew). But something happened… With our power came great responsibility (think *Spiderman*) and we blew it. We gave over the power to destruction. And we started to get smaller. So did the world. Marred, broken… is there any more accurate way to view our world today? But God had a plan for even that inevitability.

Salvation

"Salvation" is a fancy way of saying that you and I need fixing. But that's not hard to see for everyone who uses both of their eyes to look in the mirror – we all need fixing. And all of us, together, including the entire created order, need fixing – collectively. If we are going to be fixed it's going to take an idea that is larger than our problems. And that brings me back to the tattoo.

You see, the tattoo is a song all about this – a boundless salvation – because Boundless is bigger than our curse. I'm pretty tired of people who use God's plan to save us as a personal path to happiness or success or even to peace, because it's so much bigger than that. God's plan is to put right everything that's been broken in the world. Every one of His children, every one of His created beings. God's plan of salvation is a plan for the entire world – it's, well, boundless. It's bigger than me.

I remember hearing the singer Bono once asked about becoming a politician. He said he had thought about it but then remembered that when a politician gives a speech, he gives it once – maybe if it's really good people listen to it twice. But when you write a song, it becomes part of you. You feel the song. You live the song. You sing the song.

I got "Boundless" tattooed on my arm because I want to live the song. I want my life to be immersed in the message of this salvation. This message is larger than me. I want it visible. I want to embrace the pain. I want to live the promise. I want to believe with everything that I am and everything that I've got that there is a better way to live, that I can help bring this fix to the entire planet – that my life matters more than the small drama of my own feelings, family, and gifts. It matters to the earth.

This book isn't just about "steps" or "doctrine"; it's not even trying to convince you of something that will make your life happy. This book is about a song – a song big enough to tattoo on your body. But even more than that, it's a song that can get inside you and become a new way to live. That melody is beautiful. I pray that you'll hear it as we write – and embrace it as you live.[1]

William Booth's famous song (he wrote it back in

1893) is called "O Boundless Salvation". In seven verses, he develops a story of a person who grows from a limited, stunted existence into a boundless life. It's captivating! Here are the words. We're crafting this book around his story.

O Boundless Salvation

O boundless salvation! deep ocean of love,
O fullness of mercy, Christ brought from above.
The whole world redeeming, so rich and so free,
Now flowing for all men, come, roll over me!

My sins they are many, their stains are so deep.
And bitter the tears of remorse that I weep;
But useless is weeping; thou great crimson sea,
Thy waters can cleanse me, come, roll over me!

My tempers are fitful, my passions are strong,
They bind my poor soul and they force me to wrong;
Beneath thy blest billows deliverance I see,
O come, mighty ocean, and roll over me!

Now tossed with temptation, then haunted with fears,
My life has been joyless and useless for years;
I feel something better most surely would be
If once thy pure waters would roll over me.

O ocean of mercy, oft longing I've stood
On the brink of thy wonderful, life-giving flood!
Once more I have reached this soul-cleansing sea,
I will not go back till it rolls over me.

The tide is now flowing, I'm touching the wave,
I hear the loud call of the Mighty to Save;
My faith's growing bolder, delivered I'll be;
I plunge 'neath the waters, they roll over me.

And now, hallelujah! the rest of my days
Shall gladly be spent in promoting His praise
Who opened His bosom to pour out this sea
Of boundless salvation for you and for me.

William Booth (1829–1912)[2]

2

Glasses Half Empty, Half Full, and Overflowing

*I*s the glass half empty? Is something missing? Does your life come up short in comparison with friends, famous people, and characters on your favourite shows? (Here's a secret: their lives mostly suck too.)

Or is that glass just half full? Sure, you spin it positively to your friends, and even, usually, to yourself. You try to focus on the good things, the high points, the great memories, the positive aspects of your current existence. But the reality is, it is existence more than it is life. It's still only half full. Where's the rest?

Is that the best we can hope for on earth?

The short answer: No.

The longer answer? Let's go for the overflow! We'll invest the rest of these pages in showing you that half empty and half full are both less than the abundance that is available to all of us. We can each live a life of overflow!

For example:

I've been following the unfolding story of the Advent Conspiracy movement. The idea behind this movement is that Christmas is the best time to invest in things that matter most – life, love, hope, and peace, etc. And it's also about exposing the things that we often invest the most in, that don't matter at all – expensive gifts, material things, business toys – in order to feel better about ourselves.

So, out of this idea – that at Christmas we could spend less but give more – all these projects started to happen. As some followers of Jesus decided to give things that actually matter, they started to see some incredible things happen.

Water of life

One story is about an African village whose people only had a dirty source of water. The results were horrific. Since the stagnant water was dirty, everyone got sick, especially the children, whose immune systems weren't up to the challenge. Kids died there all the time because of bacteria in the water: a simple flu-like symptom would take them out. The whole village just lived with this as their fate. There wasn't anything that anyone could do.

Then the Advent Conspiracy guys heard about the village through a missionary contact and decided to do something not just about the sickness but about the source of the sickness.

They found a fresh water source by digging a well in the middle of the village. That fresh water was clean and safe to drink. It didn't take life, it gave it. And it still gives it. A whole village has been changed, and the way of life in that village has changed, too. The source of the diseases is no longer in charge: there is a new source, a source of life that is endless and clean and pure.

That's the boundless story. It's not just about another source of something to stuff into the hole in your life that eats away at you and causes your own sickness. It's about finding a brand new source, a clean and fresh source that will get rid of sickness for ever – giving you not just life but abundant life. Now, that's a gift that matters.

A cup overflows

There is a lot of ancient wisdom available to us in our pursuit of a boundless life. The world's most famous poem is called Psalm 23 and was written by a one-time shepherd named David. This version of it might be familiar to you:

> *The Lord is my shepherd, I shall not want.*
> *He makes me lie down in green pastures;*
> *He leads me beside quiet waters.*
> *He restores my soul;*
> *He guides me in the paths of righteousness*
> *For His name's sake.*
>
> *Even though I walk through the valley of the shadow*
>   *of death,*
> *I fear no evil, for You are with me;*
> *Your rod and Your staff, they comfort me.*

> *You prepare a table before me in the presence of*
> *my enemies;*
> *You have anointed my head with oil;*
> *My cup overflows.*
>
> *Surely goodness and lovingkindness will follow me all*
> *the days of my life,*
> *And I will dwell in the house of the Lord forever.*

There's heaps of juicy stuff here, but just check out the promises near the end:

God prepares a table – a feast – for him, and his enemies have to stand there and watch! Did you get that? David's enemies impotently peer in through the window and contemplate the spectacle of him enjoying a lavish spread.

God anoints his head with oil. The honoured guest in ancient times was blessed with expensive perfume, poured on the head. Besides the obvious practical element in a culture punctuated by pungent odours (of both humans and creatures), there is a powerful spiritual component to this action. His cup overflows. This signifies boundless abundance. David was living life in the overflow!

Goodness and mercy are in hot pursuit of him all the days of his life. Have you ever met that kind of person? It seems as though kindness, love, understanding, integrity, and goodwill chase them around.

And he gets to move in with God! David doesn't have to settle for some vague notions of the supernatural, resign himself to occasional warm fuzzies over coffee with close friends, dabble in the paranormal, flirt with the magical. He gets to experience G O D – and not for some fleeting instant. He moves in, settles down, changes his address, puts down roots, rearranges the furniture… This is more than divine visitation, it's a habitation.

As the King James Version of the Bible puts it, his "cup runneth over". Other versions of the poem render the phrase "my cup overflows",[3] "You fill my cup until it overflows",[4] "my cup is brimming over",[5] and "my cup overflows with blessings".[6] The original Hebrew word (*revayah*) means "saturation".

Do you get the idea?[7]

A boundless life – a life lived in overflow – is for you.

Don't settle for the unsatisfactory half-empty or half-full options. Don't settle for a contaminated source. Get the clean and boundless life. Go for the overflow.

3

Deep Ocean of Love

O boundless salvation! deep ocean of love,
O fullness of mercy, Christ brought from above.
The whole world redeeming, so rich and so free,
Now flowing for all men, come, roll over me!

Spray of the waves

I was so tired and burnt out. I felt a bit hollow inside. I needed a break, and my friend happened to live in Bermuda (a small paradise). So I took her up on an invitation to go and hang out there for a week, to try to get my breath back. After a convoluted trip (I forgot my ID!) and a longer journey than expected, I finally arrived. Even though I was in a tropical paradise, and with a dear friend, I was still weary. It seemed like the weariness wasn't coming "at" me, it was "in" me. It was in my bones.

I decided to go for a run on day two. I love running, so I strapped on my sneakers and just started to explore the place. I found a little abandoned railway track that went along the coast of the island. It was enough of a trail to run freely on, and it was breathtakingly beautiful. The waves crashed on the shores, spraying me with refreshing mist. It was epic – a stunning view.

As I was running I heard God. Now, this part sounds a bit weird. And, granted, it is hard to explain. But I heard God within me – not a voice from heaven booming down or anything dramatic like that, but a small, steady voice from inside my heart. And God said to me, "Look at the ocean." I did. It was massive. I mean, that was all you could see. Ocean. Beautiful, clear, green, and, well, huge. And then the voice spoke again: "My love for you is like that ocean."

I looked again. I felt the spray of the waves misting my sweaty body, I felt the weariness on the inside of me get showered, too. I felt the enormity of that idea – I heard the song. The love of God was like the ocean… His love for me was like *that*. Every wave was pounding at the shoreline, almost daring the earth not to move.

That water is so dangerous that it is infamous for the disappearance of ships (think Bermuda Triangle). This love isn't some sort of romantic kooky love, like you get when you hug a teddy bear. It's a fierce love. A strong love. It's deep.

As I breathed in the song, the melody got inside my heart, the tempo increasing and my heart correspondingly beating a bit faster. And I wept.

I wept because I had forgotten to sing. I had been busy working, and trying, and giving and living, but without the song. As I sat there on that cliff, I let the waves wash me. I wanted to dive right in… but I couldn't see a way out again. I sat there and let the voice, the song, the ocean, the spray wash over me. And I felt my strength return.

God loves me. Like a boundless ocean. Wave after wave after wave washed away my weariness, like a rock being pummelled into sand. Roll over me.

Ocean of love

Check out what Paul of Tarsus says about this boundless ocean:

My response is to get down on my knees before the Father, this magnificent Father who parcels out all heaven and earth. I ask Him to strengthen you by His Spirit – not a brute strength but a glorious inner strength – that Christ will live in you as you open the door and invite Him in. And I ask Him that with both feet planted firmly on love, you'll be able to take in with all followers of Jesus the extravagant dimensions of Christ's love. Reach out and experience the breadth! Test its length! Plumb the depths! Rise to the heights! Live full lives, full in the fullness of God.

God can do anything, you know – far more than you could ever imagine or guess or request in your wildest dreams! He does it not by pushing us around but by working within us, His Spirit deeply and gently within us.[8]

Open ocean swimming

This reminds me of the first time I started to train for a triathlon in open water. You see, the first and most dangerous part of a triathlon is the swimming bit. And the swim is in open water.

Too many people make the mistake of training only in a pool. But a pool is not the same as swimming in an ocean or even in a lake. The pool is measured, it's blocked off, so you don't swim in a crooked fashion. You can count the laps and kick off every fifty metres. You can swim in a straight line.

That day I had decided it was time to go for a long swim in the open ocean – I needed to get used to swimming while I navigated my direction and timed myself for distance. As I walked into the water it was the weirdest feeling. There was one guy on the beach at the time who was looking at me as strangely as I felt. I simply immersed myself in the ocean and started swimming. Where was I swimming to? I had no idea. What was the best route to take? No clue. How long was the route I'd take? Not one hint.

I was simply swimming. It was so "open", it was a bit paralysing. I was so free, I felt like I was in danger. What if a shark ate me? Would anyone even know? What if a boat came along and ran me over? What if I got lost and tired in the open ocean? I mean the whole thing was crazy.

But soon I felt the rhythm of my breath drown out the thoughts; my body got into gear and I was off. It was amazing. Here I was, one little person in a huge ocean, all by myself, swimming my heart out. When I turned around and came back – I walked out of the water at the same place I had come in – the man on the shore looked at me and said, "You're a sight for sore eyes. I didn't know where you were going!"

"Neither did I," I responded with a huge grin.

For some people the invitation into boundless salvation is like swimming for the first time in open water: overwhelming, scary, and, well, a bit weird.

But once you walk in and start swimming, it soon becomes an exhilarating and wonderful experience. It's a whole immersion kind of thing – and it's amazing.

God's intent is to bring salvation, a fullness, this boundless love, into every corner of the earth – including into our own hearts. This experience is life-changing. There is no going back.

What God wants to do is to come to wherever you are: maybe you are sitting in your living room, or reading this in a coffee shop, or perhaps you are stuck in a predicament of your own digging. It doesn't matter what your situation is – God's love never changes. God's love is boundless, His mercy is new every morning. God wants to awaken you to His love. It's free and boundless. God invites you to live in the overflow.

Heart to heart

God, please strengthen me by Your Holy Spirit – not a brute strength but a glorious inner strength – so that Christ will live in me. Help me to stand with both feet planted firmly on love. Help me to swim around for the rest of my life exploring the dimensions of Your marvellous love. Overflow me with Your fullness, please.[9]

Amen.

4

Stains are So Deep

My sins they are many, their stains are so deep.
And bitter the tears of remorse that I weep;
But useless is weeping; thou great crimson sea,
Thy waters can cleanse me, come, roll over me!

Stains in a cell

When I first encountered the pure love of God (the first time that I consciously remember), I was in a jail cell. I was a young offender, waiting in a cell, remanded in custody and facing a longer jail sentence than ever before. I was in serious trouble.

My trouble had begun years before as drugs, crime, and a life of "adventure" seemed to keep me at odds with the law. I was raised in a family who loved God and served Him, who sang the song of Boundless Salvation quite a bit, actually, but it always seemed like a pipe dream to me. I thought somehow that it was untrue – it was just a silly song to me then.

What I did know was that I was quite good at being bad. And I enjoyed the adrenaline of the chase, the high. I was quite honestly blind to how life was really going. What I thought would set me free was simply taking me to more and more enclosed spaces – it was a small life. Not just outside, but inside, too.

So there I sat in a holding cell, at the bottom of a courthouse in downtown Toronto. I was alone and still buzzing from the drugs in my body that dulled my mind, making the whole experience seem a little bit adventurous. Pathetic is what it really was – but drugs never tell you the truth.

No one is able to visit you in a holding cell, but somehow a lady from The Salvation Army managed to get in. She was a woman who knew God and who knew me. She had often come to get me from police stations at the request of my parents, who had grown too weary of the process – particularly my dad, who was much too angry to trust himself with the deed.

As she came towards me I remember thinking, "Oh, great! Here comes the lecture." A kid like me always got a lot of lectures. Comments such as "You know better", "Why are you doing this?" and the like were tiresome at best. They always made me want to disappear. No doubt truth is hard to swallow when you're stuffed with lies. Anyway, a guard opened my cell and she stepped in, and there we were. That's when it happened.

She never said anything. Shocking. I was expecting

some kind of rebuke – but nothing. She stepped forward and wrapped her arms around me and whispered in my ear, "I love you." That was it. Well, I should say that was the epic bit. I was so numb and cold that I never responded, not even to the hug. I just stood there like a dead person. As she went out I muttered, "You didn't even bring me a cigarette?" just to keep my cool. Then she was gone.

That's when He showed up. Jesus. It is the most difficult thing to try to explain. Did I see Him, or hear Him, or feel Him? I'm not sure, exactly, but I know that He came into my cell. I was alone, my friend had left me, and I was still groggy and tired from my long journey to jail. Then Jesus showed up. He did what she did – He walked towards me. No lecture. No rebuke. Just wrapped His arms around me and whispered in my ear, "I love you." And He was gone.

And everything changed. Whatever He brought with Him (boundless love?) was left with me. I don't know how it happened. But the best way to explain it was that someone had turned on a light in my cell. It was as if I had awakened from a bad dream… and suddenly I could see clearly. And now I knew that God wasn't mad at me; that He loved me. I didn't submit to His love right away – I still had some major barriers – but this vision changed everything. It changed my life from the inside out. I would never be the same again.

What Jesus brought with Him was light. Light makes everything clearer. I started to understand that sin makes our lives small – killing us with a kind of life from the wrong source.

Popsicle stains

There is a story about wolf-hunting in the extreme north of Canada, in which Eskimos repeatedly dip a sharpened knife in seal blood, creating a "bloodsicle".

The wolf's keen sense of smell identifies the bloodied knife. It licks the blood over and over, finally exposing the knife. The tongue is insensitive to the sharp edge, but the warm blood accelerates the licking. Warm blood feeds insatiable thirst until the wolf dies.

We do the same. With a ravenous appetite we gorge ourselves on the very bad habits, negative tendencies, and selfish default reactions that exacerbate our craving for more, and compound our problems.

King David wrote these words after an unusually bad season:

Generous in love – God, give grace!
Huge in mercy – wipe out my bad record.
Scrub away my guilt,
soak out my sins in Your laundry.
I know how bad I've been;
my sins are staring me down.

You're the One I've violated, and You've seen
it all, seen the full extent of my evil.
You have all the facts before You;
whatever You decide about me is fair.
I've been out of step with You for a long time,

in the wrong since before I was born.
What You're after is truth from the inside out.
Enter me, then; conceive a new, true life.

Soak me in Your laundry and I'll come out clean,
scrub me and I'll have a snow-white life.
Tune me in to foot-tapping songs,
set these once-broken bones to dancing.
Don't look too close for blemishes,
give me a clean bill of health.
God, make a fresh start in me,
shape a Genesis week from the chaos of my life.
Don't throw me out with the trash,
or fail to breathe holiness in me.
Bring me back from gray exile,
put a fresh wind in my sails!
Give me a job teaching rebels Your ways
so the lost can find their way home.
Commute my death sentence, God, my salvation God,
and I'll sing anthems to Your life-giving ways.
Unbutton my lips, dear God;
I'll let loose with Your praise. [10]

When I finally submitted my life to God it was several weeks since He had appeared to me in my jail cell. I know it doesn't seem like a smart thing to do, but even after I'd had a vision of His love for me I was scared to receive it. I was scared that I couldn't live up to it – I was so good at screwing everything up all the time that I didn't trust that I could actually do something good. And in some ways I was right.

In a few weeks I managed to get out of jail (a miracle, and another story!), but I used drugs shortly afterwards, in a familiar beginning of a downward cycle. Even I was tired of living this way. One Sunday, when someone offered a chance to pray to God I finally got up and went to kneel at a bench at the front of a house of God and gave my life to Him. I told Him that I had tried and had completely failed. This is truth.

We can all try to live a good life, but none of us will succeed. We can't do it. It's like trying to combat a poison source (like that contaminated water source in Africa) by treating the symptoms: it won't work. The source is off. We need a new source. A pure source.

So I knelt at a bench and I prayed – mostly I cried. I relinquished control over my life and gave my life to Jesus. All of it. The good, the bad, and the ugly. No more secrets. No more hiding. No more lying. He could have all of me. I finally admitted to Him (ironically, since He already knew), and to myself, and to some people who were praying for me, that I was totally broken. I was messed up. I was not a good guy. I was the bad guy. I needed God.

You and I aren't unique. We're not the only ones to find ourselves shattered. In the psalm we quoted above, King David recognized his utter helplessness and hopelessness, the deep stains of sin that splotched his life. In the words of the song, William Booth was ruined to bitter tears of remorse. Like the wolf insatiably licking itself to death, we have all ruined ourselves by our own selfish, lusty greed.

Heart to heart

Have mercy on me, O God, according to Your unfailing love; according to Your great compassion blot out my transgressions. Wash away all my iniquity and cleanse me from my sin. [11]

Amen.

5

Deliverance I See

My tempers are fitful, my passions are strong,
They bind my poor soul and they force me to wrong;
Beneath thy blest billows deliverance I see,
O come, mighty ocean, and roll over me!

Same old story

I don't know about you, but I get tired of the same old story. You know how it goes. I work with people who struggle with some very dark things. And I get tired of hearing the tragic story of their family line. It seems like "the song that never ends", except with a haunting minor-key melody that mocks a whole string of generations. "My dad was an alcoholic and I hated him for it. Now I'm an alcoholic and my son hates me."

It seems people are enslaved by their own history. Some people call it fate, and others call it their terrible destiny. In some parts of the world they use the term "karma" to explain why some people are born into such terrible circumstances. Ultimately, karma suggests that people deserve their lot in life, even if it's because of something they did in a former one.

It's an easy way to explain suffering, poverty, and loss – but it's not a very good one. It promotes an easy fatalism that is common throughout the world today. "Oh well, terrible poverty exists, and addiction, violence, and pain, and well, there's nothing really to be done about it – so everyone should just do the best they can, and on and on and on and on it goes." It sucks.

U2 wrote a song called "Grace", which suggests how Jesus interrupts and destroys karma. In it, Bono explains that Grace exists outside the principle of karma. In other words, Grace – or grace – is an interruption of the whole system of "you'll get what is coming your way". Fatalism is not the ultimate boss when you understand the boundless salvation option that Jesus offers. Karma bows to grace.

Jesus barges in on karma with a new grace – an offer to stop the vices and the generational curses that seem to be heaped upon us. He offers us a new life.

General Eva Burrows (world leader of The Salvation Army a couple of decades ago) once said this:

> *You know, if you send an alcoholic to be treated by a doctor, he becomes a healthy alcoholic. If you send him to a psychiatrist, he becomes a balanced alcoholic. If you send him to many of these programs, he becomes a sober alcoholic. But if you send him to Jesus Christ, he becomes a transformed man.*[12]

Jesus can break the cycle.

Many of us have been there. Maybe you have. It seems like an endless cycle of lack of fulfilment, failure, and self-destruction, leading to hopelessness, cynicism, and despair.

You might even be able to relate to the prisoner described by the Roman poet Virgil 2,000 years ago:

> *Having long maintained a useless conflict against*
> *innumerable hosts and irresistible might, he is at last*
> *wounded and taken prisoner; and to render his state more*
> *miserable, is not only encompassed by the slaughtered,*
> *but chained to a dead body; for there seems to be here an*
> *allusion to an ancient custom of certain tyrants, who*
> *bound a dead body to a living man, and obliged him to*
> *carry it about, till the contagion from the putrid mass*
> *took away his life.*[13]

Did you catch that? The wounded prisoner is manacled to a dead body and has to drag it around. All this time the corpse is decaying and spreading infection to its bound partner until, in the grossest imaginable manner, both shackled bodies are dead.

The Apostle Paul knew all about this. Looking back at his earlier ordeals, when his name was still Saul, he says, "What a wretched man I am! Who will rescue me from this body that is subject to death?"[14]

Have you experienced that too? Have you grown sick and tired of trudging around with the burden of expectations, regrets, grief, disappointment, and hurt, and been progressively infected with apathy, depression, pessimism, and enmity? Is it eating away at your energy, your enthusiasm, your confidence and attitude?

For some people it is a ruptured relationship. For others it is a deeply hurtful act they perpetrated in the past. Still others are stuck in neutral as they suffer some victimization over and over. Maybe you are someone who has just missed opportunities and feel the time has passed. Or you squandered your chances and are left with little to show.

You can relate.

To catch a monkey

What's one of the easiest ways to catch a monkey?[15]

1. Find a jar.
2. Fill it with peanuts.
3. Tie it to a tree (ideally a tree in an area known to be frequented by monkeys, otherwise this might not work!).
4. Wait.

That sounds easy! What apparently happens next is this:

A monkey who happens to swing by will notice the jar and go for the snack. He'll reach in to grab a handful of peanuts but get stuck trying to pull his fist out of the opening.

That monkey is stuck. At this point, you apprehend the monkey.

Now, we should warn you that the actual apprehension might get messy. The monkey, we're assured, won't let go of the tasty snack, but will be absolutely freaking out at his detention and imminent capture. But the scary shrieking (scary to both the monkey and you) won't win the monkey his freedom. He just doesn't realize that letting go of the peanuts is the only way out.

Jesus was on to the plight of this monkey, and to the predicament of you and me, when He explained, "If you try to hang on to your life, you will lose it. But if you give up your life for My sake, you will save it."[16]

Peanuts are good. But when they are in a jar hanging from a tree, be vigilant.

Here's what the Bible says about this muddle: "Do not give the devil a foothold."[17] In other words, there is an enemy of the overflow – a being, a spirit, an entity that does not want you to live. This shouldn't be news to you – at least, not if you're paying attention. There are forces at work whose role is to suck life out of the marrow of who you are.

Have you ever felt bound? Like you can't get away from an old dodgy habit or shameful practice? You aren't alone.

Teaching this idea to some kids, we actually grabbed one kid's foot and invited the boy to go on with his life. You can imagine the limitation and accompanying frustration when you're caught by a "foothold". A foothold quickly becomes a stronghold.

It's as if we say to an enemy of the overflow, "Grab hold of my foot." How stupid is that? How can we live life in overflow when something's got us by the ankles? We're stuck with it.

This foothold advice was originally given in Greek, and the word translated "foothold" is *topos*. Its first meaning is "place, any portion or space marked off, as it were from surrounding space".[18] The word probably looks familiar, related as it is to our English word "topography".[19]

There is a Salvation Army camp in Canada which is in the middle of a larger property owned by someone else. The law dictates that the owner of the land that surrounds the camp must provide a right of way for people to get to the camp from the public road.

So this means that day or night, twenty-four hours a day, every staffer, every faculty member, and every snotty-nosed youngster can cross the owner's land to and from the public road by using the right of way.

Our lives are like the larger property. And those dodgy habits and shameful practices are sometimes like the camp property within our lives. Enemies of the overflow[20] can legally come in and go out of our lives at any time through the access those habits and practices give them.

How does that happen? Well, look, the enemies of the overflow are described in Jude 6 in the Bible as being bound in "dark places" (there's the sense of topography again).[21] If you are harbouring dark places in your life, these enemies of the overflow can fester there, too.

Do you have any dark places in your life? Do you ever find yourself in a dark place? You're not alone – there are probably some enemies of the overflow hiding there with you.

What's the solution to that?

You need to shut down the camp – the disgracefulness in your life. If the enemy of the overflow has no dark places in your life in which to putrefy, it has no legal right into your life.

The thing about the monkey? *We're* the monkey. We're the ones with our hearts set on peanuts. We're the ones willing to risk our very lives for something that's nuts! We need to let go of our life. Otherwise, we're caught, just like the monkey.

We need to chop loose that dead body we've been lugging around with us for all these years.

How do we do it?

Here are some tips for shedding dead bodies, illuminating dark places, and letting go of your life. Try saying this out loud:

1. *I am sorry for my sins.* I'm genuinely full of regret for the pain I've caused, not just to every person affected but also to You, God.

2. *Please forgive me.* I want release from the deadness of my own wrongdoing.

3. *I renounce these sins* [by name, out loud]. I want nothing to do with these terrible things I've done [bad habits] any more.

4. *I command* the spirit of [the specific enemy of the overflow behind the repented sin – for example, lust, hate, laziness, greed] to leave, in Jesus' name, to go where Jesus commands you, and never to return.

5. *Holy Spirit, please fill me up.* Like a big ocean, come and drench me on the inside. Refresh my life and then immerse me in Your love, healing, truth, and power. Saturate me with Your goodness.

6. *Please protect me from the enemy.* Close my life to any connection I may have with the enemy of the overflow.

Heart to heart

Jesus, You came to destroy the works of the enemy of the overflow.[22] *I submit to You; I resist the devil, and I'll watch him flee from me.*[23] *Amen.*

6

Joyless and Useless

Now tossed with temptation, then haunted with fears,
My life has been joyless and useless for years;
I feel something better most surely would be
If once thy pure waters would roll over me.

*H*elen[24] seems to have it all together. She's a successful lawyer from a great school making heaps of cash, married to a fantastic guy who is also witty and attractive and Christian. And yet Helen is disillusioned.

You'd think she'd be experiencing overflow.

I mean – elite education, sensational job, rich, healthy, and even Christian!

How can Helen still be empty?

We're warning you, the answer is ugly. It is not pleasant to look at because it may hit a bit too close to home. Helen complains that at week's end, at every week's end, all she sees is work, groceries, and laundry. One of the most brilliant people we know, and all she's got to show for her living is work, groceries, and laundry.

You can see how this frustrates, dissatisfies, and leaves discontent.

This is not the Boundless overflow we are talking about. This is settling for a poor imitation.

Bluntly, the solution for Helen is surrender. Full surrender. Yes, Helen gave her heart to Jesus when she was young. Yes, she faithfully attends her place of worship, and "does her bit" for the congregation. Yes, she reads her Bible, and prays. Jesus has forgiven Helen's sins, adopted her into His family.

She's going to heaven. But it's on her terms, not Jesus' terms. Helen has simply added Jesus to an already busy life. She lives and does what she wants, and she adds Jesus to the mixture in the hope that He will satisfy her deepest desires. But that's not the invitation Jesus makes. Jesus suggests (as we have already read) that we are to join Him in a global movement of change. Our whole lives become centred around Jesus – we don't just try to fit Jesus into a life of our own choosing.

Helen has the potential to impact eternity. She could be living life in the overflow right now. Of course, it would require a different lifestyle. It would require a radical re-posturing of her life to surrender everything to Jesus. She needs to fully surrender control of her life and be filled with Holy Spirit.

Currently, there are limits to her commitment. Right now, there is a framework in which Helen allows God to work. God can't fit our human frameworks – He's just not that small. When she starts eating, sleeping, and breathing Jesus, He'll be free to transform her. The key change with full surrender will be the Holy Spirit filling her.

The Holy Spirit will invade her whole being, filling her with love, joy, peace… He can transform her immense talents into powerful gifts that can be used effectively for His glory – when she lets Him have control, it'll be boundless.

The Holy Spirit also fills the void, the discontent of an endless string of weeks full only of work, groceries, and laundry. No longer are disillusionment and dissatisfaction the hallmarks of her life. This is how she plunges into a Boundless salvation.

Can you relate to Helen? Sure, it might not come out over the phone, or in public. But when you reflect on the weeks and months, what do you have to show for them? Why not surrender, fully? Let the Holy Spirit saturate you and let Him set the agenda.

Eternal life

Then it happened that a man came up to Him and said, "Master what good thing must I do to secure eternal life?" "I wonder why you ask Me about what is good?" Jesus answered Him. "Only one is good. But if you want to enter that life you must keep the commandments." "Which ones?" he asked. "'You shall not murder,' 'You shall not commit adultery,' 'You shall not steal,' 'You shall not bear false witness,' 'Honour

*your father and your mother', and 'You shall love your
neighbour as yourself'," replied Jesus. "I have carefully
kept all these," returned the young man. "What is still
missing in my life?"*

*Then Jesus told him, "If you want to be perfect,
go now and sell your property and give the money away
to the poor – you will have riches in Heaven. Then
come and follow Me!" When the young man heard that
he turned away crestfallen, for he was very wealthy.
Then Jesus remarked to His disciples, "Believe me, a
rich man will find it very difficult to enter the kingdom
of Heaven. Yes, I repeat, a camel could more easily
squeeze through the eye of a needle than a rich man get
into the kingdom of God!" The disciples were simply
amazed to hear this, and said, "Then who can possibly
be saved?" Jesus looked steadily at them and replied,
"Humanly speaking it is impossible; but with God
anything is possible!"*[25]

Annie and coming into Jesus

I was privileged to know a woman named Annie.[26] Annie
was one of 6,000 drug-addicted residents of the downtown
eastside of Vancouver, Canada's poorest postal code. She
was what they called "dual diagnosis", which meant simply
that she was mentally ill and drug-addicted. Annie had
dreadlocks and wild eyes. She was always a bit unkempt
(think dirty and long fingernails). If you ran into her on the
street you'd possibly be a little frightened.

Every now and then Annie would end up with a free trip to a psychiatric ward. On one such occasion I went to visit her, and as we were walking among the beautiful grounds of the hospital Annie turned to me and said, "Isn't it wonderful the way Rob turned into Jesus?"

I was a bit speechless.

Rob, you see, was a friend of ours who had met Jesus as a heroin addict. Jesus healed him and saved him, and Rob was an incredible example of someone who lived a boundless life. But now we had confused poor Annie. We were trying to help her, and it seemed we had just added to her delusions. I thought I should correct her wrong assumption, so I said, "Well, Annie. Rob is like Jesus. But really, Rob invited Jesus to come into his life." Annie looked at me with some pity and said, "Yes. But when Jesus came into Rob, didn't Rob also come into Jesus?" Wow. I stood corrected.

The thing Annie understood is a key part of what it means to *realize* the boundless salvation we've been talking about. You see, we often treat Jesus and His message of salvation like something small for our own personal lives. As if salvation were simply about us feeling better or feeling forgiven. Those things are true, but they're not the whole truth. The whole truth is that we are invited out of our small lives and into something larger. When Jesus comes into us, we are also invited to come into Him: He's that *big*. And that is a totally different way to live. When Jesus encountered the disciples, He invited them to follow Him.

He didn't ask if He could spend the rest of His life with them as a fisherman or tax collector. He invited them to leave their lives to follow Him – He was asking them if they wanted to be part of the plan to save the entire created order. He was asking if they wanted to live the boundless life with Him. This is still the invitation.

Jesus isn't begging us to let Him into our lives – He doesn't "need" us to feel good about Himself. He loves us and created us to be part of a plan to impact and change the earth – and the call to live a boundless life is to leave our small plans (however grand they might have been or sounded to us) for His plans, which are infinitely bigger. A friend of ours wrote a song with this sentiment, which includes this important line: "Thank You for showing me the emptiness of all I held onto… I surrender my life, I surrender my everything to You."[27]

Jesus once told a story that depicts the predicament:

"[The kingdom of heaven] is also like a man going off on an extended trip. He called his servants together and delegated responsibilities. To one he gave five thousand dollars, to another two thousand, to a third one thousand, depending on their abilities. Then he left. Right off, the first servant went to work and doubled his master's investment. The second did the same. But the man with the single thousand dug a hole and carefully buried his master's money.

"After a long absence, the master of those three servants came back and settled up with them. The one

*given five thousand dollars showed him how he had
doubled his investment. His master commended him:
'Good work! You did your job well. From now on be
my partner.'*

*"The servant with the two thousand showed how
he also had doubled his master's investment. His master
commended him: 'Good work! You did your job well.
From now on be my partner.'*

*"The servant given one thousand said, 'Master, I
know you have high standards and hate careless ways,
that you demand the best and make no allowances for
error. I was afraid I might disappoint you, so I found
a good hiding place and secured your money. Here it is,
safe and sound down to the last cent.'*

*"The master was furious. 'That's a terrible way
to live! It's criminal to live cautiously like that! If you
knew I was after the best, why did you do less than the
least? The least you could have done would have been
to invest the sum with the bankers, where at least I
would have gotten a little interest.*

*"'Take the thousand and give it to the one who
risked the most. And get rid of this "play-it-safe"
who won't go out on a limb. Throw him out into utter
darkness.'"*[28]

(There's that bit about dark places again.)

William Booth is describing that last servant when he
writes, "Now tossed with temptation, then haunted with

fears, my life has been joyless and useless for years."

Maybe he is describing you, too?

On the face of it, I suspect we would all rather be Helen than Annie. But Helen is stuck if she responds to Jesus in the way the wealthy young man in the previous story did. And in comparison, Annie is a $1,000 servant. But she ran with what she had and saw Jesus in ways many of us never do. I reckon that during those seasons when Annie wasn't tormented by her "dual diagnosis", her life was punctuated by more than just groceries and laundry.

God has given you gifts and abilities. He is their source. If you choose to hold on to them, you're positioning yourself downstream of temptation and fears, and setting yourself up for joylessness and uselessness. If you surrender control of everything – including your gifts and abilities, your time and passions, your resources and future – to the Lord Jesus Christ, He'll partner with you (that's what it says in the story!) in a boundless life that enables you to live in the overflow.

Heart to heart

Lord, I surrender. Everything. Come into me as I come into You. Roll Your pure waters over me. And I will follow You, all the way to heaven.

Amen.

7

Ocean of Mercy

O ocean of mercy, oft longing I've stood
On the brink of thy wonderful, life-giving flood!
Once more I have reached this soul-cleansing sea,
I will not go back till it rolls over me.

The climb

I remember the idea being a good one. My friend
Denise and I were excited to include in our whitewater
rafting trip another exhilarating event: bungee
jumping. The great idea is to strap your feet together to a
giant bungee cord and jump off a bridge to "feel" you are
falling until the bungee cord "catches" you, so to speak, and
you allow the adrenaline to fill every part of you.

As I said, it was a good idea. And it would have been a
cool thing just to be able to run over the side of the bridge
and jump to freedom. But this set-up was different: what you
had to do was to climb a massive ladder to a small bridge
that was attached to a giant crane. Step by step you had to
keep climbing up. And what was a good idea at the start

became an increasingly difficult thing to actually do.

The slow climb was enough to drain the enthusiasm out of the best of us. Once you got to the top of the 300-foot climb you waited on a small precipice as someone strapped your feet into a harness, and then you shuffled your way to the edge of the bridge and waited for your name to be called. By the time you got to the jump you were a little less than ready! You see, the problem wasn't the jump, it was the climb. Climbing slowly to the inevitable jump is not the best way to be spontaneous in your quest for adrenaline rushes.

Many of us struggle with this when it comes to making a decision to follow Jesus. We count the steps, we chart out the potential course, we take our time – inching our way to the precipice where we must jump into the ocean. We miss the beauty of spontaneity, and this can result in making the jump much harder. The thing about my bungee jumping experience is this: once I was out on the precipice, shuffling along the side of it, waiting for my turn, it was very hard not to jump. In order *not* to jump I'd have had to shuffle my way back to the base, get someone to unshackle me from my various restraints and pieces of apparatus, and then climb back down the 300-foot ladder that I had just climbed up. Simply put, the best route out of that situation was to jump.

Lots of people handle life the same way they enter the water – they tentatively inch out, hanging around the shallows so their bodies can adjust to the temperature. They wait too long and miss opportunities. Salvation is ultimately an act of faith – it requires a decision, and then a jump. The faith needed to enter into the boundless ocean of God's great love is simple: you need to trust that God will catch you.

Go join a circus?

Author and teacher Henri Nouwen once travelled with a circus for an entire year to learn how God works. I'm not joking. He travelled with a circus community to study God. He was most struck by the relationship between the trapeze artists, who, he figured, really represented the way we relate and interact with God. Nouwen explained that people think the most important member of the trapeze team is the middle one who does all the fancy flips and tricks and lets go and then is caught on the other end, in a dazzling display of death-defying stunts, putting his or her very life on the line.

But in the actual composition of the trapeze team, the "most valuable player" – the one everyone knows is crucial – is the catcher. The catcher ensures that the middle player has the faith to make the jump. The faith of the middle trapeze artists is not in their ability to make the jumps (although they must have that as well). Their faith is in the catcher's ability to catch them.

But if we don't come to trust the catcher – if we don't make the jump, if we don't relinquish control and throw ourselves into the great sea – we will miss the experience. We will not fly. And this is where it's important to pay attention: we must fix ourselves to never turn back. We must determine in our hearts and minds to make the dive – to make the jump and allow the Catcher (the most important member of our team) to make the catch and allow us the opportunity to be free to make the jump.

We can stand on the shoreline of this great salvation for our whole lives, trying to summon up the courage to take the plunge. The reassuring news is that those who do summon up the courage, in Phil Wall's words, "worship a God who is constantly lapping at the shores of people's lives".

He's there, ready.

What holds you back?

What are you afraid of?

Do you know the Catcher?

Do you know others who have "jumped"?

How to survive an anaconda attack

If you've been on the internet since the 1990s, you may remember receiving this in your inbox. It may be an urban legend.[29]

The following is from the US Government Peace Corps Manual for its volunteers who work in the Amazon jungle. It tells what to do if an anaconda attacks you. (It assumes you have a sharp knife!)

1. If you are attacked by an anaconda, do not run. The snake is faster than you are.

This first instruction is a little bit crazy. I don't know about you, but my first instinct if I were to see a large snake in a jungle would be to run. I would run like the wind, actually. But if I were to run I would most likely die. So I carry on reading the instructions.

2.   Lie flat on the ground. Put your arms tight against your sides, your legs tight against one another. Stay completely still.
3.   Tuck your chin in.
4.   The snake will come and begin to nudge and climb over your body.

Ummm. Okay. Now I'm freaking out. A giant snake is nudging and climbing over my body! What? Who wrote this? How do they know the outcome? Someone has done this before?

5.   Do not panic.

Please see my comments above. I've already begun to panic. Actually, in reality I'm already dead in this situation, as my legs would have run before my brain could instruct them otherwise.

6.   After the snake has examined you, it will begin to swallow you from the feet and always from that end. Permit the snake to swallow your feet and ankles. Do not panic.

Okay. Do not panic. Stay completely still. Let the snake eat you. What? Does any of this sound familiar? Many people I know have lain down and allowed the enemy to swallow them. Slowly, the enemy of the overflow just begins to swallow up joy, hope, life, freedom: inch by inch the enemy swallows our essence. We become snake food.

7. The snake will now begin to suck your legs into its body. You must lie perfectly still. This will take a long time.

Again, it can take years. One day we look in the mirror and we hardly recognize ourselves. Is that us? Did we intend to grow old and indifferent? Grouchy and proud? Did we become the very person we said we'd never turn into? Did we mean for the grudge to turn into a rift? Did we think the bitterness could go that deep? Did we ever expect to feel so alone?

8. When the snake has reached your knees, slowly and with as little movement as possible reach down, take your knife and very gently slide it into the side of the snake's mouth between the edge of its mouth and your leg, then suddenly rip upwards.

This is the boundless salvation action. The part where the story turns, where what looked as though it was going to die actually lives. I know this isn't a true instruction, but seriously: this is some good news – finally. The snake doesn't have to win, even when it thinks it's got us swallowed whole. We can move. Suddenly. We can dive into an ocean, we can unsheathe a knife, we can cut that snake and get it off our bodies – and we can walk away. We can live. We can have the very thing we were always meant to have: we can be saved.

The word of God is the most effective knife there is. It's described as "sharper than a two-edged sword" and it has the power to separate joints and marrow, and soul and spirit.[30] It's intense. It's exactly what's needed to kill a snake that tries to devour you! I have this incredible idea: instead of succumbing to death, instead of just lying down for the rest of our lives and allowing the snake to consume us, we should get active. Why not grab the sword of God and strike the enemy with this blow: "Jesus has come to give us life, and life to the full"?[31]

"So then, be very careful how you live. Don't live like foolish people but like wise people. Make the most of your opportunities because these are evil days."[32]

Some people have their lives all mapped out. They want to go to this university and marry this person and get that job and live in this city… We've talked about how futile our own plans can be. We've come to realize that God has a lot more in store for us if we'll submit to His direction.

Others fail to plan at all. They meander aimlessly through life and miss out on all kinds of experiences and opportunities because they failed to prepare. Be very careful how you live. Don't live like foolish people, but like wise people.

You just don't know when you'll get this opportunity again. I once met a guy on a bus leaving an evangelistic event in a big city. It turned out that I knew some people he knew, and we settled in to discuss the evening's meeting. I tried to clarify the good news about Jesus dying on the cross for his sins, how Jesus conquered sin and death when He rose back to life, how He defeated the devil, how He ascended to heaven, how He is interceding right now for him and me, and how He plans to return to earth. But my new friend didn't buy it. He had issues he had to think about.

Through our mutual friends I heard that he had died in an accident a couple of days later. I drove to his city for the funeral. You know the kind. Everyone was saying what a great guy he was and how now he was in a better place – in heaven. I was disturbed by this since I'd talked to him just a few days earlier and he had rejected the good news of the Lord Jesus Christ, refusing to repent of his sins and follow Jesus.

A family member noticed me and approached. She told me that this guy had spoken with her about the preaching, our conversation, and the invitation of Jesus, and that he had decided to turn from his sins and accept Jesus' invitation into His life. She assured me that the celebration in the funeral was legitimate, that he was indeed in heaven.

What if he'd put it off for a few more days?

You just don't know when you'll get this opportunity again…

Heart to heart

I trust You to catch me. I won't turn back. I'm going to take the plunge into Your boundless love, mercy, grace, forgiveness, and joy. Help me to use Your sword of salvation to slice the enemy off me. Catch me!

Amen.

8

Plunge 'Neath the Waters

The tide is now flowing, I'm touching the wave,
I hear the loud call of the Mighty to Save;
My faith's growing bolder, delivered I'll be;
I plunge 'neath the waters, they roll over me.

As they make music they will sing, "All my fountains are in you."[33]

The monster is me

ne of the best stories I've ever read is *Les Misérables* by Victor Hugo. I love it. Jean Valjean is the main character, a poor guy who gets arrested for stealing a loaf of bread for his hungry family. He is wronged. And then he goes to jail.

In jail the wrong that was done to him becomes a wrong inside him. He gets bitter and jaded and becomes much like the men who surround him – more like an animal than a man. When he finally gets out of prison he finds a bishop's house and asks for help. The bishop is a man a lot like Jesus and gladly helps him: he feeds him, gives him shelter – treats him like a human.

In the middle of the night Jean Valjean gets up and steals all the silverware and takes off. The police catch him and return him to the bishop's house, and then something remarkable happens. The bishop says, "Oh yes – I'm so glad you returned, because you forgot the candlesticks!" And instead of calling Jean a thief and getting him sent to jail, the bishop blesses him with more.

The next few pages in the story are remarkable. Something happens *inside* Jean Valjean that can't quite be explained. He says that what happened was that the love and grace he received from the bishop exposed a darkness and ugliness inside him. He realized that the monster he so hated was not the jail, the men, or the sentence – it was himself.

He was the monster. He fell to his knees and began to weep over the ugliness inside him – and as he did that, he felt the love of God enter him.

This is a deep truth. When we finally glimpse the love and beauty of God, it illuminates our own ugliness. It exposes the darkness in our own lives – our sin. And that should give us reason to cry. For the things we want to blame our unhappiness on are not the real problem – the problem is inside us.

Until we realize this we will never live in the overflow. But when we do come to it we are made new. We enter a boundless ocean… "Come, roll over me!"

And what comes with that ocean is remarkable – it's the power and ability to change a life. It's the incredible grace and mercy of a king who extends His offer of mercy where there should have been judgment. We are invited to dine at a table and have our fill. We don't have to be hungry for the rest of our lives for something we can't have: we can be filled to the brim with the best of food, things we've been longing for throughout our lives – peace, love, joy, acceptance, forgiveness, grace, mercy, and truth. We can be set free.

Booth calls God "mighty to save", and He is. I've seen God take very broken people and transform them into examples of wholeness – the very people the world can discard are taken into this amazing ocean and transformed into pearls of His grace and love.

Every week an outreach team composed of women in our Christian community visit exotic massage parlours. We visit the women there to let them know that someone is interested in who they are and in any needs they might have. From referrals to a listening ear and to prayers, we are "chaplains" to the invisible women behind the shaded windows of sex for sale.

On a recent visit to one massage parlour we were met at the front door by the owner/worker, who said, "Thank God you are here!" She took us to the back waiting area and introduced us to a "colleague" of hers who was in need. The woman told us a bit of her story of addiction and deadness, and finally turned to us and asked, "I need forgiveness, healing and freedom: can you help me?" Great question. It made me wonder how many more women are asking the same question, even in the silence. My friend, who has journeyed through some similar things, shared her own story of how God took her from being an angry, desperate, addicted woman to freedom – so free that now she could go and help others. That very moment I was able to introduce that lovely young woman to Jesus, and her journey to freedom began. God is able to do things we can't even imagine. Once you are touched by this incredible force of love, something inside you changes. You become new – you become, well, really alive for the first time.

In the Greek language there are a couple of words for life – one is *bios* (from where we get the word "biology") and the other is *zoe*. The difference between them is important. One is physical life and the other is spiritual life. Jesus said that He came that we might have life and have it to the full. What He meant was that He came so that we might be fully alive, not just in body or in mind but in spirit – our passions, our energies, our life totally engaged with the Spirit of life. And that's what this ocean does. It wakes us up *inside*. It brings life where there has been deadness, healing where there has been pain, freedom where there has been slavery. This ocean is flowing indeed: once you touch that kind of life you never want to turn back – you want the ocean to push you over. It generates within you a tenacity of spirit that longs for what is possible…

Blind Bart

Then they came to Jericho. As Jesus and His disciples,
together with a large crowd, were leaving the city, a blind
man, Bartimaeus (which means "son of Timaeus"),
was sitting by the roadside begging. When he heard that
it was Jesus of Nazareth, he began to shout, "Jesus,
Son of David, have mercy on me!"

Many rebuked him and told him to be quiet, but
he shouted all the more, "Son of David, have mercy on
me!"

Jesus stopped and said, "Call him."

So they called to the blind man, "Cheer up! On
your feet! He's calling you." Throwing his cloak aside,
he jumped to his feet and came to Jesus.

"What do you want me to do for you?" Jesus
asked him.

The blind man said, "Rabbi, I want to see."

"Go," said Jesus, "your faith has healed you."
Immediately he received his sight and followed Jesus
along the road.[34]

Blind Bart – have mercy on me. Shhh. Embarrassing us
– making a spectacle, bringing attention to us, bothering
Jesus…

In order to receive the salvation that Jesus has
promised, in order to enter a new way of living, we must
be willing to plunge in. We've got to be willing, like Blind

Bart, to abandon ourselves to His great purposes. Blind Bart was getting nowhere with his dignity. His dignity was only serving to help with his condition – he was still blind.

His healing was linked to a lot of other things. His ability to work and make an income, to be eligible to marry someone, to be thought of as a contributing member of society, to provide for his family – all depended on being able to see, so he had a deep desire to be healed. When he heard that Jesus was in town he began to cry out – so much so that it embarrassed his family and friends.

This is important to mention: sometimes your desire for freedom, healing, and deliverance will be embarrassing for some others close to you. They want you to pretend that everything is fine. But deep down you know it isn't. Everything isn't fine: you are falling apart inside. You are hurting and lonely and broken, and you need some help.

Everything else in your life hinges on this. Don't let pride and dignity have the final say over whether you can be free. Get undignified if you must – shout out, say a prayer, kneel down where you are and ask Jesus to heal, save, redeem you, regardless of the consequences. Let the ocean roll over you.

Salvation for the weak

My friend Sarah[35] was a prominent city official and a strong, confident woman. She was a professor who ran her own programme at the local college, and a city council member. She was brilliant at networking and had contacts throughout the town. I asked her for some help in a campaign I was running for The Salvation Army to raise some much-needed money for an outreach programme.

She agreed (mainly because it would help her public profile when she ran for mayor), but only on the condition that I understood something. She wanted me to understand that she thought religion was for "the weak".

When she told me that, I was relieved. You see, sometimes people try to tell others that religion/salvation is for confident, strong, able people – but it isn't. Jesus said that it was for the broken, the weak, the blind, the lame, and the suffering. So I simply replied to my friend that I was so glad she understood salvation and that I was the weakest of the Christians. Jesus wasn't just a crutch, He was my wheelchair. Apart from Him I'd most likely be dead.

She was flustered by my response. She went home and wrote a long apology email to me saying that she hadn't meant to insult me and that she didn't see me as weak (we played basketball together and I'm not exactly weak on the court!). I told her that to admit my weakness was no insult – it's a fact. And that everyone who comes to Jesus must acknowledge their deep need of Him.

A few months went by and the fundraising campaign went really well. But one day Sarah called me and asked to meet me. We met in a little shop for a mid-morning coffee and Sarah blurted out, "I'm soooo weak!" She began to weep.

Through her tears and emotion she told me of the

weakness she had learned to stuff down, deep inside, because she had come from a high-achieving, albeit dysfunctional, family who prided themselves on strength and confidence. Sarah oozed self-confidence and success in her life, but she longed for meaning and purpose deep inside.

Inside she felt dirty, lost, broken, and alone. She felt, well, dead. As soon as she got honest and embraced her weakness, we could pray. And pray we did. Sarah dived into a deep ocean of forgiveness, love, mercy, and peace and she was saved that day. She entered into a new way of being.

Today she is mayor of that town. And instead of lording it over her people, she is affectionately recognized as a leader who cares, who listens, who is generous and compassionate, who isn't afraid to cry at tragedy and laugh at hilarity. She is fully alive. What a joy to see her swim in the open ocean of God's great salvation.

Instead of pretending, like Sarah, wouldn't it be better to simply admit your need and take the plunge?

Instead of running like Valjean, wouldn't it be better to acknowledge your sin, as he did, and fall on the mercy of a gracious God?

Instead of accepting a small life of condemnation and restriction, wouldn't it be better, like Blind Bart, to cry out to the God who exists, who cares, and who has the power to intervene in your life?

He hears. He forgives. He accepts. He loves. He restores. He regenerates. He saturates. He invigorates. As you plunge 'neath the waters, they *will* roll over you.

Heart to heart

All my fountains are in You. Please save me from my pride. Show me the deep stains within me. I admit the monster is inside me. Please wash me, heal me, and clean me from the inside out. I'm weak and needy. The tide is now flowing. I'm touching the wave. I plunge 'neath the waters…

Amen.

9

Boundless Salvation

And now, hallelujah! the rest of my days
Shall gladly be spent in promoting His praise
Who opened His bosom to pour out this sea
Of boundless salvation for you and for me.

Banana-flavoured medicine

My second son developed an ear infection once and required some antibiotics. That's a normal situation, but he was only two. And two-year-olds are never normal. His favourite phrase at the time was "No way!" and he used it all the time.

So I managed to get some banana-flavoured medicine from the doctor. It was in liquid form and I had a syringe ready for him. I told him that monkeys loved the medicine and they were trying to get it from me, so he'd better take it as fast as possible. He said, "No way!" Trying to think quickly, I said, "Forget the monkeys; the tigers love this so much they try to eat the monkeys who eat this medicine – it's that amazing!" He said, "No *way!*"

I pleaded with him, and then I tried to bribe him. I did a little dance and made monkey noises and lots of different animal sounds, and, well, he said, "*No way!*" So I did what every loving and kind-hearted parent on the planet would do – I held that little kid down. I wrestled him to the floor and got my older son to hold his head still while I shoved the medicine down his throat. You see, he needed to get better. In spite of himself.

Sometimes I'm tempted to do the same thing with salvation. I'm tempted to try to entertain you, to disguise the medicine with banana flavouring – to sugar-coat the truth so you will swallow it. I'm tempted to dance and sing and make animal noises – to plead with you to take it. The reason why I'm tempted to do this is that I know salvation is the cure for your sickness. I know that only Jesus has the remedy for what ails you. And if you don't get it – you will eventually die.

But the thing is that Jesus *never* did that. The Bible *doesn't* do that. Ever. Sure, it's all true. But it's bigger than that. Salvation isn't just about you. It's about the entire planet. Salvation is about God restoring everything created to what it was always supposed to be. Think of every wrong righted, every thing that's crooked put back straight – think of the earth full of goodness!

That is God's salvation plan: every person being their best self. You see, salvation, at least the boundless kind that Jesus offers, isn't in the form of a syringe that you have to take or else. It's in the form of an ocean, full of truth, beauty, and love, and Jesus simply invites you to dive in – take the plunge, live the adventure. And the choice is yours. This Jesus will always give you: a choice. Because true love always does. So you choose.

Vladimir

Vladimir Mikhailovich was only sixteen years old when he took the plunge. In St Petersburg, Russia, he met Jesus and was never the same again. He loved everything about salvation and was keen to learn, to read the Bible, and to follow Jesus. Soon he was playing the cornet in a Salvation Army band in Moscow at the time when Stalin took over control of the Soviet empire.

He suddenly found himself arrested because of his public Christian stand and sentenced to prison. Sixty men to a thirty-bed cell in a hidden, infamous jail right in the centre of Moscow. He was only seventeen years old and was stuck with murderers, thieves, and some pretty bad men. He didn't know what to do. He was so afraid every day, and having just become a Christian he didn't know the Bible well enough to defend his faith, so the dominant prisoner in his cell used to mock him and his beliefs.

Every day Vladimir would take a burnt match and write out this petition on a scrap of paper: "Please send Bible: Vladimir Mikhailovich, cell 5." He would wet his bread and hide the piece of paper inside it, then wait until the bread had dried overnight and the message couldn't be seen. Then when he was working in the yard, when the guards weren't looking he would throw the bread over the wall and pray to God, "Please, God, let someone find this who will send me a Bible – then I can defend my salvation!"

Every day he did this, month after month. His evil cellmate continued the abuse, and Vladimir got close to breaking. One evening, when the bully was starting to pick on Vladimir and rough him up again for his "stupid faith", a guard came to the door with a package for Vladimir.

Now in prison in Moscow the security system was not exactly high tech. On the contrary, all they did to ensure there were no weapons in the packages was cut them in four pieces. Everything sent to the prison was cut in four before being delivered to the prisoners.

So Vladimir grabbed the package but was shaking so violently from fear that he dropped the package and it fell to the cell floor. The paper opened and revealed a fish cut in four pieces. As the pieces opened, there in the middle of the fish lay, uncut and whole, a Bible!

The murdering, mocking cellmate fell to his knees and exclaimed, "There is a God." That night in that cell in the centre of Moscow a seventeen-year-old boy led fifty-nine thieves and murderers to the boundless ocean of salvation. Jesus was their new friend. Everything changed for every one of them.

Later that evening they were all sent to solitary confinement for singing hymns too loudly – but Vladimir said that was fine, because he could still hear the singing from his solitary cell. That night Vladimir discovered that his salvation was bigger than him and that his whole life could be an adventure in the open water of boundless salvation.

Sure he could live a predictable "lap life" in the safety of the swimming pool, counting the time, measuring every action, staying in the right lane and safe from all harm – or he could go for the open-water swim and live the adventure, albeit a dangerous one. He could be saved all the way through.

When I met Vladimir he was eighty-eight years old and had lived adventure after adventure after adventure. He was still up for it at that age after a life of the most punishing labour camps and prisons. He had seen Jesus show up in places and in ways that most of us only dream about. He had understood and embraced salvation, and it showed through his every word, story, and example. He sings this verse of William Booth's song with tears streaming down his face – because it's true. Every. Word. Is. True.

Vladimir took the ocean option and would gladly sing the salvation story anywhere, any time, at any price, because he caught the song. He sings it with his life.

I've joined him. I remember taking a train ride back to Moscow after interviewing Vladimir and hearing story after story of this incredible life adventure. And I remember saying, "I want to live like that." I want to live the song.

So if you are tempted to pretend you have it all together, and accept some small syringe of just enough salvation to save you but leave you the same, you'll miss the point of the song and of this book and what Jesus came for. He came to save you – not just you, but the whole world.

All the way through

"He [Jesus] is able to save completely those who come to God through Him."[36]

Yes, Jesus can save people from ultimate destruction. But He wants to do so much more than that. He wants to save you from yourself, from sin, from despair, from brokenness, from hopelessness, and more…

"Jesus came to save you from your sins, not in them."[37]

You can experience more than forgiveness of your sins. You can enjoy victory over them. You can experience more than triumph over temptation. You can revel in transformed desires so that a lot of those temptations are neutered.

He is able to save "completely" – to the uttermost, absolutely, throughout, all the way through (as different versions of the Bible express it) – or as John Wesley used to say, from "all the guilt, power, root, and consequence of sin."

He can saturate you. He can neutralize your natural inclination to act selfishly. He can overflow you with the Holy Spirit. He can accompany you through a boundless life lived in overflow. It sounds almost too good to be true, but it isn't. It's the gospel truth. My friend from the Caribbean testifies to this truth with a wonderful accent and a life story as well. "When Jesus saved me," she says, "He saved me – all the way through." Thank God.

Heart to heart

Fill me to the measure of all Your fullness, please. Saturate me. I want You to enable me to live life in overflow. Save me all the way through. I'm Yours.

Amen.

10

Overflow

On the final and climactic day of the Feast, Jesus took
His stand. He cried out, "If anyone thirsts, let him come
to me and drink. Rivers of living water will brim and
spill out of the depths of anyone who believes in me this
way, just as the Scripture says."[38]

This is it! This is the overflow – brimming and
spilling. Several versions of the Bible say, "Out of
his belly will flow rivers of living water."

What is this living water? Jesus was talking about the
Holy Spirit filling you up and then overflowing, splashing,
and washing all over your world.

Picture the setting. We're in the temple in Jerusalem
and it is one of the high and holy days on the Jewish calendar
– the Feast of Tabernacles.

As far as we can tell, each night of the feast has been
an all-nighter – partying and celebrating all night long. And
then each morning a procession of priests has headed to the
pool of Siloam to draw water. When they returned, to the

accompaniment of the choir chanting Psalms 113–118 and great joy all around, they poured out the water over the altar as a sacrifice.

There are all kinds of prophetic fulfilment in this stuff, but on the last and greatest day of the feast they are performing this exercise *seven* times. And it is at this climactic moment, the seven celebratory pourings over the altar, that Jesus stands up.

In the midst of the joyous cacophony, He needs to shout to be heard: "If anyone is thirsty, let him come to me and drink." He is fulfilling exactly what they are celebrating (as well as numerous Bible texts, including Proverbs 8; Isaiah 49:10 and 55:1).

And His invitation epitomizes what is available to you and me, today. Living life in overflow is coming to Jesus and drinking, and drinking, and drinking, until we're filled up and rivers of living water flow out of our belly.[39]

Are you up for it?

We aren't trying to convince you to tattoo "O Boundless Salvation" on your wrist. But we'd love you to tattoo it on your heart.

May your life sing the story until Jesus comes back.

Until then, our prayer is that "by the power of the Holy Spirit you may abound and be overflowing".[40]

Heart to heart

Lord, I believe. I receive. Fill me, please. I want to overflow with Your Holy Spirit and live a boundless life into eternity. Amen.

Postscript

Reading *Boundless: Living life in overflow* is a start. But there are other things that you can do to help you position yourself downstream in the river of God's grace, so that you overflow and bubble over. Here are a few:

- **Live in community** – find some keen followers of Jesus where you live and live life alongside them.
- **Read the Bible** – God communicates with us in heaps of ways (the topic of another book), but the main means, and the standard for measuring every other means, is the Bible. I read it every day. You'll benefit if you do too.
- **Pray** – converse with God. This is our *Heart to heart* bit. He speaks with us. But we also speak with Him. Why not try to open a conversation with Him now, that doesn't stop until Jesus comes back?
- **Get discipled** – this is critical. Salvation is not just a decision to follow Jesus – it *is* following Jesus. Find someone who can help direct your path on the Jesus way. The way that this boundless salvation is "the whole world redeeming" is by multiplying disciples of the Lord Jesus Christ. This happens intentionally within Christian community. Once you join one, seek someone to disciple you.

If you need help connecting with some of these things, check out the links and resources at the end.

11

Boundless Overflow

We've just scratched the surface when it comes to Boundless and Overflow in the Bible. Here is a taste of some more…

Boundless

Psalm 147:5
Great is our Lord and of great power; His understanding is inexhaustible and boundless. (Amplified Bible)

John 3:34
For since He Whom God has sent speaks the words of God [proclaims God's own message], God does not give Him His Spirit sparingly or by measure, but boundless is the gift God makes of His Spirit! (Amplified Bible)

Ephesians 3:8
To me, though I am the very least of all the saints (God's consecrated people), this grace (favor, privilege) was granted and graciously entrusted: to proclaim to the Gentiles the unending (boundless, fathomless, incalculable, and

exhaustless) riches of Christ [wealth which no human being could have searched out]. (Amplified Bible)

Ephesians 6:10
In conclusion, be strong in the Lord [be empowered through your union with Him]; draw your strength from Him [that strength which His boundless might provides]. (Amplified Bible)

1 Peter 1:3
Praised (honored, blessed) be the God and Father of our Lord Jesus Christ (the Messiah)! By His boundless mercy we have been born again to an ever-living hope through the resurrection of Jesus Christ from the dead. (Amplified Bible)

Ephesians 1:15–19
That's why, when I heard of the solid trust you have in the Master Jesus and your outpouring of love to all the followers of Jesus, I couldn't stop thanking God for you – every time I prayed, I'd think of you and give thanks. But I do more than thank. I ask – ask the God of our Master, Jesus Christ, the God of glory – to make you intelligent and discerning in knowing Him personally, your eyes focused and clear, so that you can see exactly what it is He is calling you to do, grasp the immensity of this glorious way of life He has for His followers, oh, the utter extravagance of His work in us who trust Him – endless energy, boundless strength! (The Message)

Psalm 119:96

To all perfection I see a limit; but Your commands are boundless. (New International Version)

Overflow

John 10:10

The thief comes only in order to steal and kill and destroy. I came that they may have and enjoy life, and have it in abundance (to the full, till it overflows). (Amplified Bible)

Psalm 45:1

My heart overflows with a goodly theme. (Amplified Bible)

Proverbs 3:10

So shall your storage places be filled with plenty, and your vats shall be overflowing with new wine. (Amplified Bible)

Joel 2:24

And the [threshing] floors shall be full of grain and the vats shall overflow with juice [of the grape] and oil. (Amplified Bible)

Romans 15:13

May the God of your hope so fill you with all joy and peace in believing [through the experience of your faith] that by the power of the Holy Spirit you may abound and be overflowing (bubbling over) with hope. (Amplified Bible)

2 Corinthians 2:4

For I wrote you out of great sorrow and deep distress [with mental torture and anxiety] of heart, [yes, and] with many tears, not to cause you pain but in order to make you realize the overflowing love that I continue increasingly to have for you. (Amplified Bible)

2 Corinthians 7:4

I have great boldness and free and fearless confidence and cheerful courage toward you; my pride in you is great. I am filled [brimful] with the comfort [of it]; with all our tribulation and in spite of it, [I am filled with comfort] I am overflowing with joy. (Amplified Bible)

Colossians 2:7

Have the roots [of your being] firmly and deeply planted [in Him, fixed and founded in Him], being continually built up in Him, becoming increasingly more confirmed and established in the faith, just as you were taught, and abounding and overflowing in it with thanksgiving. (Amplified Bible)

1 Thessalonians 3:12

And may the Lord make you to increase and excel and overflow in love for one another and for all people, just as we also do for you. (Amplified Bible)

2 Chronicles 29:31–32

Everyone in the congregation brought sacrifices and Thank-

Offerings and some, overflowing with generosity, even brought Whole-Burnt-Offerings, a generosity expressed in seventy bulls, a hundred rams, and two hundred lambs – all for Whole-Burnt-Offerings for God! (The Message)

Psalm 104:24–30

What a wildly wonderful world, God! You made it all, with Wisdom at Your side, made earth overflow with Your wonderful creations. Oh, look – the deep, wide sea, brimming with fish past counting, sardines and sharks and salmon. Ships plow those waters, and Leviathan, Your pet dragon, romps in them. All the creatures look expectantly to You to give them their meals on time. You come, and they gather around; You open Your hand and they eat from it. If You turned Your back, they'd die in a minute – Take back Your Spirit and they die, revert to original mud; Send out Your Spirit and they spring to life – the whole countryside in bloom and blossom. (The Message)

John 16:23–24

"This is what I want you to do: Ask the Father for whatever is in keeping with the things I've revealed to you. Ask in My name, according to My will, and He'll most certainly give it to you. Your joy will be a river overflowing its banks!" (The Message)

James 3:17–18

Real wisdom, God's wisdom, begins with a holy life and is characterized by getting along with others. It is gentle and reasonable, overflowing with mercy and blessings, not hot one day and cold the next, not two-faced. You can develop a healthy, robust community that lives right with God and enjoy its results only if you do the hard work of getting along with each other, treating each other with dignity and honor. (The Message)

Romans 5:15
But the gift is not like the trespass. For if the many died by the trespass of the one man, how much more did God's grace and the gift that came by the grace of the one man, Jesus Christ, overflow to the many! (New International Version)

2 Corinthians 1:5
For just as the sufferings of Christ flow over into our lives, so also through Christ our comfort overflows. (New International Version)

2 Corinthians 4:15
All this is for your benefit, so that the grace that is reaching more and more people may cause thanksgiving to overflow to the glory of God. (New International Version)

Questions You
May Have

*B*efore you are willing to plunge into the boundless overflow we're describing, you may have a few questions that need addressing.

Does God exist?

We're making an assumption in the main text of the book that you acknowledge that God exists. In case you aren't sure, here is one approach and some links with more information:

Cause and effect: "Out of nothing, nothing comes." So everything that begins to exist has a cause. What caused the universe? According to popular understanding – the "big bang" – there was no matter and no time at the start of the universe. God is described in the Bible as being "spirit" (no matter) and eternal (no time). He fits the conditions. What caused God? Well, since He is eternal, He didn't have a start and doesn't require a "cause".

Here's a helpful site: reasonablefaith.org (William Lane Craig).

Who is Jesus?

We're describing Jesus as key to the whole boundless life. And lots of people have different views on who Jesus was and is. Some think He was a prophet, others a religious teacher, some a founder of a religion, and so on. We believe that He is God. Here's one reason why:

C. S. Lewis described a thing called the Christian trilemma. It goes like this:

Jesus claimed to be God. Either it is true or it isn't true.

Let's consider the possibilities if it isn't true. Either He knows it isn't true, or He doesn't know it isn't true. Got it?

If He knows it isn't true, we have a guy who deceivingly claims to be something He is not – God. He's a liar.

If He doesn't know it isn't true, we have someone falsely claiming to be God and actually believing that He is! He's deluded – a lunatic.

Let's go back to the original dilemma – either it is true or it isn't true. We've considered the only options if it isn't true. The other possibility is that it is true – that he claimed to be God and it is true. What does that make Him? Lord.

So, Lewis explains that we have only three options for who Jesus is – Lord, liar, or lunatic. If you look into Him some more, you'll conclude, as we have, that He's far from the latter two options.

Here's a helpful site: josh.org (Josh McDowell).

Is the Bible reliable?

We're basing our description of the boundless life on the Bible. Some people aren't sure of the Bible. Here's why we rely on it:

The Bible is not a geography textbook. But it is entirely accurate geographically, including obscure details such as the directions of winds at certain times of the year and the title of the chief on a minor island.

The Bible is not a history textbook. But it is entirely accurate on details of history, including obscure details that research continues to confirm as it advances.

The Bible is not a science textbook. But it is entirely accurate scientifically, predating scientific theory on all kinds of basic things, such as the fact that the earth is a sphere, light is in motion, every star is different, air has weight, blood is the source of life.

The Bible is a prophetic book, and unlike every other "holy" book or sacred text or prophetic or fortune-telling volume it is entirely accurate – none of the 2,000+ prophecies in the Bible have been wrong.

For these and many more reasons, the Bible is reliable – we can trust what it teaches.

Here's a helpful site: reasons.org (Hugh Ross, and source of the scientific stuff we've alluded to here).

What about the problem of evil?

We're pitching evil as an enemy of the overflow and we know that it sometimes trips people up when it comes to full surrender to God. Here's our quick take:

Love is the highest good. Love is possible only within the framework of free will. That is, you need to be able to choose to love for it really to be love. Otherwise you are just a robot. But the best possible world – one that provides opportunity to choose to love – also provides the option to choose not to love, to choose evil. The potential of evil is a ramification of making the highest good possible. God treats us as people, not as robots. And the negatives of that treatment pile up.

Here's a helpful site: rzim.org (Ravi Zacharias and friends).

We're just scratching the surface on this stuff. But Craig, McDowell, Ross, and Zacharias can help you go deeper if you have more questions.

Author Resources

Danielle Strickland has the following titles:

Salvationism 101 with Stephen Court
Chaotic Order
Just Imagine with Campbell Roberts
Challenging Evil with Carvosso Gauntlett
The Liberating Truth

Stephen Court has these titles:

Salvationism 101 with Danielle Strickland
Be a Hero with Wesley Campbell
Proverbial Leadership with Wesley Harris
Revolution with Aaron White
The Uprising with Olivia Munn
One Thing with Jim Knaggs
One Day with Jim Knaggs
One Army with Jim Knaggs
Hallmarks of the Salvation Army with Henry Gariepy
Holiness Incorporated with Geoff Webb and Rowan Castle
Boston Common (editor)
Greater Things with James Thompson
Army on its Knees with Janet Munn
High Counsel with Joe Noland
A Field for Exploits with Eva Burrows

@StephenCourt twitter
And you can contact us on Facebook.

Notes

1. We aren't trying to convince you to tattoo "O Boundless Salvation" on your wrist, but we'd love you to tattoo it on your heart.

2. Commissioner Theodore Kitching said that on arriving one day at the Founder's home at 6:00 a.m., he found William Booth completing the verses of this song, which he had written during the night. It was apparently first sung at "Boundless Salvation" meetings in Exeter Hall, London, on 14–15 November 1893. The verses, with a chorus "The Heavenly gales are blowing", were published under the title "Boundless Salvation" in *The War Cry* on 23 December 1893. William Booth announced this song when he appeared in public for the last time at his eighty-third birthday celebrations in the Royal Albert Hall, London, on 9 May 1912. (See Robert J. Morgan, *Then Sings My Soul*, Nashville: Thomas Nelson, 2011, p. 129.)

3. New International Version.

4. Contemporary English Version.

5. James Moffatt.

6. New Living Translation.

7. Now, don't forget that there is much more in Psalm 23. It's worth a lot of consideration.

8. This is from The Message version of Paul's letter to the Ephesians, chapter 3, verses 14–21.

9. This prayer is based on Ephesians 3:16–19.

10. This is from The Message version of Psalm 51, verses 1–15.

11. This prayer is from the New International Version of Psalm 51, verses 1–2.

12. General Eva Burrows, "In the Front Line", *The Empire Club of Canada Addresses*, 6 October 1988, pp. 62–71.

13. "Virgil paints this in all its horrors, in the account he gives of the tyrant Mezentius. Aeneid, lib. viii. ver. 485." *Clarke's Commentary on the Bible*.

14. This is from the New International Version of Paul's letter to the Romans, chapter 7, verse 24.

15. There are several versions of this story floating around. This is ours.

16. This is from the New Living Translation of the Gospel according to Matthew, chapter 16, verse 25.

17. This is from the New International Version of Paul's letter to the Ephesians, chapter 4, verse 27.

18. This is from the Blue Letter Bible site: http://www.blueletterbible.org/lang/lexicon/Lexicon.cfm?strongs=G5117

19. This is from the Apple Dictionary entry for "topography": the arrangement of the natural and artificial physical features of an area: *the topography of the island*; a detailed description or representation on a map of such features.

20. We're using this term to refer to demons.

21. This is from the New Life Version of Jude 6. It is notably related to our topographical allusion in that the first part of the verse speaks of "angels who did not stay in their *place* of power, but left the *place* where they were given to stay" (our italics).

22. This is based on John's first letter, chapter 3, verse 8.

23. This is based on James's letter, chapter 4, verse 7.

24. This is not her real name.

25. This is from J. B. Phillips's translation of the Gospel according to Matthew, chapter 19, verses 16–26.

26. Annie is her real name!

27. This is from the excellent song "I Surrender", by Phil Laeger, at phillaeger.com. It is used by permission.

28. This is from The Message version of the Gospel according to Matthew, chapter 25, verses 14–30.

29. This version is from urbanlegends.about.com.

30. This is from the letter to the Hebrews, chapter 4, verse 12.

31. This comes from Jesus, in the Gospel of John, chapter 10, verse 10.

32. This comes from the God's Word Translation version of Paul's letter to the Ephesians, chapter 5, verses 15–16.

33. This comes from the New International Version of Psalm 87, verse 7.

34. This comes from the New International Version of the Gospel according to Mark, chapter 10, verses 46–52.

35. Sarah is not her real name.

36. This comes from the New International Version of the book of Hebrews, chapter 7, verse 25.

37. Catherine Booth.

38. This is from The Message version of the Gospel according to John, chapter 7, verses 37–38. Verse 39 reads: "(He said this in regard to the Spirit, whom those who believed in him were about to receive. The Spirit had not yet been given because Jesus had not yet been glorified.)"

39. The Feast of the Tabernacles context from the IVP Commentary, as well as this elaboration:

In Jewish writings water is a very rich symbol (cf. Goppelt 1972:318–22). God himself can be called "the spring of living water" (Jer 2:13; 17:13). Other texts that use water imagery speak of Wisdom (Baruch 3:12; Sirach 15:3; 24:21, 25–27, 30–31), the law (Sifre on Deuteronomy 48) and, as here in John 7:39, the Holy Spirit (Genesis Rabbah 70:8; Targum of Isaiah 44:3). Jesus, in offering the Spirit (v. 39), is claiming to be able to satisfy people's thirst for God. The cries of the psalmists are answered. David prayed, "O God, you are my God, earnestly I seek you; my soul thirsts for you, my body longs for you, in a dry and weary land where there is no water" (Ps 63:1). The sons of Korah sang, "As the deer pants for streams of water, so my soul pants for you, O God. My soul thirsts for God, for the living God. When can I go and meet with God?" (Ps 42:1–2). http://www.biblegateway.com/resources/commentaries/IVP-NT/John/Jesus-Source-Living-Water-All

40. This is from the Amplified Version of Paul's letter to the Romans, chapter 15, verse 13.